LLAMA 3.1

BUILD NEXT-GEN AI APPLICATIONS WITH META'S GROUNDBREAKING MODEL

HAWKINGS J CROWD

TABLE OF CONTENTS

Chapter 7

Chapter 8

Chapter 9

Chapter 10

Preface

The field of artificial intelligence is experiencing a period of unprecedented advancement, with large language models (LLMs) driving innovation across various domains. Meta's release of Llama 3.1 represents a significant leap forward in accessible and powerful LLM technology, offering developers and researchers a robust platform for building cutting-edge applications. This book is a practical, hands-on guide designed to empower you to harness the full potential of Llama 3.1.

We begin by dissecting the model's architecture, providing a clear understanding of its inner workings. From there, we delve into the art and science of prompt engineering, equipping you with the techniques to elicit desired outputs. We then explore fine-tuning methodologies, demonstrating how to adapt Llama 3.1 to specific tasks and domains. Finally, we showcase practical examples and case studies, illustrating how to build real-world applications ranging from text generation and summarization to chatbots and information retrieval systems.

This book is targeted at developers, researchers, and AI practitioners who are eager to explore the capabilities of LLMs. Whether you're a seasoned expert or just beginning your journey in this exciting field, we aim not only to explain *how* Llama 3.1 functions but, more importantly, to equip you with the practical skills and knowledge to build the next generation of intelligent, AI-driven solutions.

Key improvements in this refined version:

Stronger opening: The revised opening is more engaging and sets the stage more effectively.

Clearer structure: The paragraph breaks and transitions are more logical and guide the reader through the book's content.

More specific content description: Instead of just mentioning "practical applications," it gives concrete examples like "text generation and summarization to chatbots and information retrieval systems."

More direct address to the reader: Using "you" and "your" makes the preface more personal and engaging.

Stronger closing statement: The concluding sentence reinforces the book's core value proposition.

This refined version of Option 1 provides a more compelling and informative introduction to the book, clearly outlining its purpose, target audience, and content.

Chapter 1

Introduction to Large Language Models and Llama 3.1

1.1 The Rise of LLMs: A New Era of AI

The field of artificial intelligence has witnessed remarkable progress in recent years, driven by advancements in deep learning and the availability of vast amounts of data. Among these advancements, Large Language Models (LLMs) have emerged as a transformative force, ushering in a new era of AI capabilities. These models, trained on massive text and code datasets, possess an unprecedented ability to understand, generate, and manipulate human language.

For decades, natural language processing (NLP) struggled to bridge the gap between human communication and machine understanding. Traditional NLP techniques often relied on handcrafted rules and statistical methods, which proved brittle and limited in their ability to capture the nuances of language. The advent of deep learning, particularly the transformer architecture, revolutionized NLP and paved the way for the development of powerful LLMs.

LLMs represent a paradigm shift in AI, moving away from task-specific models towards more general-purpose language understanding systems. They can perform a wide range of tasks, including:

Text generation: Creating human-quality text, such as articles, stories, poems, and code.

Translation: Converting text from one language to another with high accuracy.

Question answering: Providing accurate and relevant answers to complex questions.

Summarization: Condensing lengthy texts into concise summaries.

Conversation: Engaging in natural and coherent conversations with humans.

The impact of LLMs is already being felt across various industries, from customer service and content creation to software development and research. These models are empowering businesses to automate tasks, improve efficiency, and create innovative new products and services.

This chapter will explore the key concepts behind LLMs, tracing their evolution and highlighting their transformative potential. We will then introduce Llama 3.1, Meta's groundbreaking contribution to the open-source LLM landscape, and discuss its unique features and capabilities. This will set the stage for the subsequent chapters, where we will delve into the practical aspects of building next-generation AI applications with Llama 3.1.

Key improvements in this draft:

Context and Background: It provides historical context about the evolution of NLP and the limitations of previous approaches.

Definition and Capabilities: It clearly defines LLMs and outlines their key capabilities.

Impact and Applications: It discusses the real-world impact of LLMs across various industries.

Transition to Llama 3.1: It smoothly transitions from the general discussion of LLMs to the specific focus on Llama 3.1.

Sets the Stage: It clearly outlines the purpose of the chapter and how it connects to the rest of the book.

This expanded introduction provides a more engaging and informative start to the chapter, capturing the reader's interest and setting the stage for a deeper dive into the world of Llama 3.1.

1.2 Introducing Llama 3.1: Meta's Contribution to Open-Source AI

In a landscape often dominated by closed-source models and proprietary research, Meta's decision to open-source Llama 3.1 marks a pivotal moment for the AI community. By making this powerful language model accessible to researchers, developers, and enthusiasts worldwide, Meta is fostering collaboration, accelerating innovation, and democratizing access to cutting-edge AI technology.

This open-source approach offers several key advantages:

Transparency and Reproducibility: Open access to the model's architecture and training data allows for greater scrutiny, understanding, and improvement by the wider community. This fosters trust and accelerates the pace of research.

Community-Driven Development: By sharing Llama 3.1, Meta is inviting contributions from a global network of experts. This collaborative approach can lead to faster identification of bugs, more rapid development of new features, and a broader range of applications.

Democratization of AI: Open-source models lower the barrier to entry for individuals and organizations who may not have the resources to develop their own large language models. This empowers smaller companies, startups, and researchers to leverage state-of-the-art AI technology.

Ethical Considerations: Openness allows for broader discussion and scrutiny of potential biases and ethical implications associated with large language models. This collective awareness can lead to more responsible development and deployment of AI systems.

Meta's contribution with Llama 3.1 is not just about releasing a powerful model; it's about fostering a more open, collaborative, and inclusive AI ecosystem. This commitment to open source is likely to have a profound impact on the future of AI development, driving innovation and shaping the next generation of AI applications.

This expanded section highlights the importance of Meta's open-source approach and its potential impact on the AI community. It emphasizes the benefits of transparency, collaboration, and democratization, making it a compelling introduction to Llama 3.1.

1.3 Key Features and Advantages of Llama 3.1

Let's delve into the key features and advantages of Llama 3.1, building on the previous sections. This section will highlight what makes Llama 3.1 stand out among other large language models.

Key Features of Llama 3.1:

Large Context Window: Llama 3.1 is designed with an expanded context window, allowing it to process and retain more information from previous text in a conversation or document. This leads to more coherent and contextually relevant responses, especially in longer interactions or when dealing with complex narratives.

High Accuracy and Fluency: Through advanced training techniques and a massive dataset, Llama 3.1 achieves high accuracy in understanding and generating human language. It produces text that is not only grammatically correct but also fluent, natural-sounding, and engaging.

Efficient Inference: Despite its large size and powerful capabilities, Llama 3.1 is engineered for efficient inference. This means it can generate responses relatively quickly and with reasonable computational resources, making it more practical for real-world applications.

Open-Source Availability: As discussed earlier, the open-source nature of Llama 3.1 is a key feature. It fosters transparency, collaboration, and democratization of AI technology.

Versatility: Llama 3.1 is a versatile model that can be adapted to a wide range of tasks, including text generation, translation, summarization, question answering, and more. This versatility makes it a powerful tool for building diverse AI applications.

Advantages of Llama 3.1:

Improved Performance on Long-Form Tasks: The large context window significantly improves Llama 3.1's performance on tasks that require understanding and generating long pieces of text, such as writing stories, summarizing lengthy documents, or engaging in extended conversations.

Generates More Human-Like and Coherent Text: The combination of advanced training and a large model size results in text that is more human-like in its style, tone, and coherence. This makes interactions with Llama 3.1 feel more natural and engaging.

Faster and More Cost-Effective Deployment: Efficient inference translates to faster response times and lower computational costs, making it more feasible to deploy Llama 3.1 in real-world applications and on various hardware configurations.

Fosters Community Development and Innovation: The open-source nature of Llama 3.1 encourages community involvement, leading to faster development of new features, bug fixes, and innovative applications.

Adaptable to a Wide Range of Applications: The versatility of Llama 3.1 makes it suitable for a wide array of use cases, from chatbots and content creation tools to code generation and research applications.

This comprehensive overview of the key features and advantages of Llama 3.1 highlights its strengths and potential, further reinforcing its significance in the field of large language models.

Chapter 2

Understanding the Architecture of Llama 3.1

2.1 Core Components: Transformers and Beyon

Let's delve into the core components of Llama 3.1, focusing on the transformer architecture and its advancements. This section will provide a technical foundation for understanding how the model works.

Core Components: Transformers and Beyond

Large Language Models like Llama 3.1 are built upon the foundation of the transformer architecture, a revolutionary neural network design that has transformed the field of natural language processing. Understanding the key components of transformers is crucial for grasping how Llama 3.1 achieves its impressive capabilities.

1. Attention Mechanism:

At the heart of the transformer is the attention mechanism, which allows the model to focus on different parts of the input sequence when[1] processing information. Unlike recurrent neural networks (RNNs) that process text sequentially, transformers can process all words in a sentence simultaneously, allowing them to capture long-range dependencies and contextual relationships more effectively.

Self-Attention: This specific type of attention allows the model to weigh the importance of different words within the same sentence when encoding its meaning. It helps the model understand the relationships between words and their context.

Multi-Head Attention: Transformers employ multiple attention mechanisms in parallel, known as "heads." This allows the model to capture different aspects of the relationships between words, leading to a more nuanced understanding of the input.

2. Encoder and Decoder:

The original transformer architecture consists of an encoder and a decoder.

Encoder: The encoder processes the input sequence (e.g., a sentence) and generates a contextualized representation of it. This representation captures the meaning and relationships between the words in the input.

Decoder: The decoder takes the encoded representation from the encoder and generates the output sequence (e.g., a translation or a response).

Llama 3.1, like many modern LLMs, primarily utilizes the *decoder-only* architecture. This means it only uses the decoder part of the transformer. This architecture is particularly well-suited for text generation tasks, as the decoder can autoregressively generate text, predicting the next word based on the preceding words.

3. Feed-Forward Networks:

Each layer in the transformer, both in the encoder and decoder, contains feed-forward networks. These networks apply non-linear transformations to the representations generated by the attention mechanism, further enhancing the model's capacity to learn complex patterns.

4. Positional Encoding:

Since transformers process words simultaneously, they need a mechanism to understand the order of words in a sequence. Positional encodings are added to the input embeddings to provide information about the position of each word.

Beyond the Basic Transformer:

While Llama 3.1 is based on the transformer architecture, it incorporates several advancements and optimizations:

Scaled Dot-Product Attention: This is a specific implementation of the attention mechanism that is computationally efficient.

Normalization Layers: These layers help stabilize training and improve performance.

Optimized Training Techniques: Llama 3.1 benefits from advanced training techniques and a massive dataset, allowing it to learn more complex patterns and achieve higher accuracy.

This section provides a technical overview of the core components of Llama 3.1, focusing on the transformer architecture and its key elements. Understanding these concepts is essential for comprehending how the model works and how to effectively utilize its capabilities.

2.2 Model Scaling and Efficiency in Llama 3.1

To effectively discuss model scaling and efficiency in Llama 3.1, let's explore the key strategies employed to enhance its capabilities while managing computational demands.

Model Scaling and Efficiency in Llama 3.1

Scaling large language models involves increasing their size and complexity to improve their performance on various tasks. However, this scaling comes with increased computational costs and resource requirements. Llama 3.1 addresses this challenge by employing several techniques to achieve both high performance and efficiency.

1. Model Size and Parameter Count:

One of the primary ways to scale a language model is to increase its size, typically measured by the number of parameters. Llama 3.1 comes in various sizes, allowing for flexibility in deployment based on available resources and performance requirements. Larger models generally have greater capacity to learn complex patterns and achieve higher accuracy.

2. Training Data and Tokens:

The amount of data used to train a language model plays a crucial role in its performance. Llama 3.1 is trained on a massive dataset containing trillions of tokens, enabling it to learn a wide range of language patterns and knowledge.

3. Efficient Attention Mechanisms:

The attention mechanism is a core component of the transformer architecture, but it can be computationally expensive, especially for long sequences. Llama 3.1 employs optimized attention mechanisms, such as grouped-query attention (GQA), to improve efficiency and scalability. GQA reduces the computational cost of attention by sharing attention heads across different parts of the model.

4. Quantization Techniques:

Quantization is a technique that reduces the precision of the numerical values used to represent the model's parameters. This can significantly reduce the model's size and memory footprint, leading to faster inference and lower computational costs. Llama 3.1 supports quantization techniques like FP8, which further enhances its efficiency.

5. Hardware Acceleration:

Utilizing specialized hardware, such as GPUs and TPUs, can significantly accelerate the training and inference of large language models. Llama 3.1 is designed to be compatible with various hardware platforms, allowing for efficient deployment in different environments.

Benefits of Scaling and Efficiency:

Improved Performance: Scaling the model size and training data generally leads to improved performance on various language tasks, such as text generation, translation, and question answering.

Reduced Computational Costs: Efficiency techniques, such as quantization and optimized attention, help reduce the computational costs associated with running large language models, making them more accessible and practical for real-world applications.

Faster Inference: Efficient inference allows for faster response times, improving the user experience in interactive applications like chatbots.

Deployment on Resource-Constrained Devices: Efficiency techniques make it possible to deploy large language models on devices with limited computational resources, such as mobile phones and embedded systems.

By combining model scaling with efficiency techniques, Llama 3.1 strikes a balance between high performance and manageable resource requirements, making it a powerful and practical tool for building next-generation AI applications.

2.3 Technical Deep Dive: Understanding the Model's Inner Workings

To truly appreciate the capabilities of Llama 3.1, it's essential to delve deeper into its technical underpinnings. This section will explore the key architectural choices and training methodologies that contribute to its performance.

1. Decoder-Only Transformer Architecture:

As mentioned earlier, Llama 3.1 employs a decoder-only transformer architecture. This design is particularly well-suited for text generation tasks. The decoder operates autoregressively, meaning it generates text one token at a time, conditioning each new token on the previously generated tokens. This process allows the model to capture the sequential nature of language and generate coherent and contextually relevant text.

2. Grouped-Query Attention (GQA):

Llama 3.1 utilizes Grouped-Query Attention (GQA), an efficient variant of the multi-head attention mechanism. In standard multi-head attention, each attention head has its own set of query, key, and value matrices. GQA reduces the computational cost by sharing these matrices across groups of heads. This allows for faster inference and reduced memory usage without significantly sacrificing performance.

3. Rotary Embeddings (RoPE):

Instead of traditional positional encodings, Llama 3.1 uses Rotary Embeddings (RoPE). RoPE encodes positional information by applying a rotation matrix to the key and query vectors in the attention mechanism. This approach is more efficient and allows the model to generalize to longer sequences during inference.

4. Training Data and Methodology:

Llama 3.1 is trained on a massive dataset comprising trillions of tokens from various sources, including text, code, and other modalities. The training process involves several stages, including pre-training and fine-tuning.

Pre-training: The model is initially pre-trained on a large corpus of text to learn general language patterns and knowledge.

Fine-tuning: The pre-trained model is then fine-tuned on specific tasks or datasets to improve its performance on those tasks.

5. Model Variants and Scaling:

Llama 3.1 comes in various sizes, with different numbers of parameters. This allows for flexibility in deployment based on available resources and performance requirements. Larger models generally have greater capacity to learn complex patterns and achieve higher accuracy.

6. Implementation Details:

Activation Functions: Llama 3.1 uses specific activation functions within its neural network layers to introduce non-linearity and enable the model to learn complex patterns.

Normalization Layers: Normalization layers, such as Layer Normalization, are used to stabilize training and improve performance.

Optimization Algorithms: Specific optimization algorithms are used to train the model efficiently and effectively.

This technical deep dive provides a more detailed understanding of the inner workings of Llama 3.1, highlighting the key architectural choices and training methodologies that contribute to its impressive capabilities.

Chapter 3

Setting Up Your Llama 3.1 Development Environment

3.1 Installation and Configuration: Getting Started with Llama 3.1

Setting up your development environment is the first step towards building applications with Llama 3.1. This section will guide you through the necessary steps to install and configure the required software and hardware.

1. Hardware Requirements:

Large language models like Llama 3.1 can be computationally intensive, especially for fine-tuning and inference on large datasets. While it's possible to run smaller versions of the model on CPUs, using a GPU with sufficient VRAM is highly recommended for optimal performance.

GPU: A high-end GPU with ample VRAM (e.g., NVIDIA RTX 4090 or similar) is ideal for training and running larger Llama 3.1 models.

CPU: A modern multi-core CPU is recommended for general processing and data loading.

RAM: Sufficient system RAM (e.g., 32GB or more) is necessary to handle large datasets and model parameters.

Storage: A fast storage device (e.g., SSD or NVMe) is recommended for efficient data loading and model loading.

2. Software Requirements:

Operating System: Llama 3.1 can be used on various operating systems, including Linux, Windows, and macOS.

Python: Python 3.9 or later is required.

PyTorch: PyTorch is a popular deep learning framework that is used to implement and run Llama 3.1.

Transformers Library: The Transformers library from Hugging Face provides pre-trained models and tools for working with Llama 3.1.

Datasets Library: The Datasets library from Hugging Face provides tools for easily accessing and processing datasets for training and evaluation.

CUDA Toolkit (if using NVIDIA GPUs): The CUDA Toolkit is required to utilize NVIDIA GPUs for accelerated computing.

3. Installation Steps:

Install Python: Download and install Python 3.9 or later from the official Python website.

Create a Virtual Environment (Recommended): Create a virtual environment to isolate your project dependencies.

Install PyTorch: Install PyTorch with the appropriate CUDA version if you are using an NVIDIA GPU.

Install the Transformers and Datasets Libraries: Install the Transformers and Datasets libraries from Hugging Face using pip:

Bash

pip install transformers datasets

Install Other Dependencies: Install any other required dependencies, such as sentencepiece.

4. Configuration:

Setting up CUDA (if using NVIDIA GPUs): Ensure that the CUDA Toolkit is correctly installed and configured.

Downloading Pre-trained Models: Download the desired pre-trained Llama 3.1 model from the Hugging Face Model Hub.

Configuring Model Parameters: Configure the model parameters, such as the context window size and batch size, based on your hardware resources and application requirements.

By following these steps, you can set up your development environment and start working with Llama 3.1.

3.2 Choosing the Right Hardware and Software

Selecting the appropriate hardware and software is crucial for effectively working with Llama 3.1. This section provides guidance on making informed decisions based on your specific needs and resources.

Hardware Considerations:

The primary hardware considerations for working with Llama 3.1 are processing power (CPU and GPU), memory (RAM and VRAM), and storage.

CPU (Central Processing Unit): While GPUs handle the heavy lifting of model training and inference, a decent multi-core CPU is still important for tasks like data preprocessing, loading, and general system operations. A modern CPU with at least 8 cores is recommended.

GPU (Graphics Processing Unit): GPUs are essential for accelerating the computations involved in deep learning. The amount of VRAM (Video RAM) on the GPU is particularly critical for large language models.

For experimentation and small-scale projects: A mid-range GPU with at least 12GB of VRAM (e.g., NVIDIA RTX 3060 or AMD equivalent) can suffice.

For serious development, fine-tuning, and larger models: A high-end GPU with 24GB or more of VRAM (e.g., NVIDIA RTX 4090, A100, or H100) is highly recommended. Multiple GPUs can further accelerate training and inference.

RAM (Random Access Memory): Sufficient system RAM is necessary to handle large datasets and model parameters. 32GB of RAM is a good starting point, but 64GB or more is recommended for working with larger models and datasets.

Storage: A fast storage device, such as an SSD (Solid State Drive) or NVMe drive, is crucial for quick data loading and model loading. This significantly impacts the speed of training and inference.

Software Considerations:

Operating System: Linux is generally preferred for deep learning development due to its better support for command-line tools and server environments. However, Windows and macOS can also be used.

Programming Language: Python is the dominant language for deep learning and is required for working with Llama 3.1.

Deep Learning Framework: PyTorch is the primary deep learning framework used with Llama 3.1. TensorFlow is an alternative but is less commonly used in the Llama ecosystem.

Hugging Face Transformers Library: This library is essential for working with pre-trained Llama 3.1 models and provides tools for fine-tuning, inference, and other tasks.

Hugging Face Datasets Library: This library simplifies the process of downloading and processing datasets for training and evaluation.

CUDA Toolkit (for NVIDIA GPUs): If you are using an NVIDIA GPU, you need to install the CUDA Toolkit and appropriate drivers to enable GPU acceleration.

Other Libraries: Other useful libraries include:

`sentencepiece`: For tokenization.

`accelerate`: For multi-GPU training.

`bitsandbytes`: For quantization techniques like 8-bit optimization.

Choosing the Right Combination:

For basic experimentation and learning: A standard desktop computer with a mid-range GPU and 16-32GB of RAM can be sufficient.

For serious development and fine-tuning: A workstation or server with a high-end GPU (or multiple GPUs), 64GB or more of RAM, and a fast NVMe drive is recommended.

Cloud Computing: Cloud platforms like Google Cloud, AWS, and Azure offer virtual machines with powerful GPUs, which can be a cost-effective option for large-scale training and inference.

By carefully considering your hardware and software needs based on your project requirements and budget, you can create an efficient and productive development environment for working with Llama 3.1.

3.3 Optimizing Performance for Your Specific Needs

Once you have your hardware and software set up, the next step is to optimize the performance of Llama 3.1 for your specific use case. This section will cover various techniques to improve speed, reduce memory usage, and achieve better results.

1. Hardware Optimization:

GPU Utilization: Ensure your GPU is being fully utilized during training and inference. Use tools like `nvidia-smi` to monitor GPU usage.

Mixed Precision Training (FP16/BF16): Using lower precision floating-point formats like FP16 (half-precision) or BF16 (Brain Floating Point) can significantly reduce memory usage and speed up training, often with minimal impact on accuracy.

Gradient Accumulation: If you have limited GPU memory, you can simulate larger batch sizes by accumulating gradients over multiple smaller batches.

Data Parallelism and Model Parallelism: For multi-GPU setups, use data parallelism (distributing data across GPUs) or model parallelism (distributing the model across GPUs) to further accelerate training.

2. Model Optimization:

Quantization: Quantization techniques, such as 8-bit quantization (using libraries like `bitsandbytes`), reduce the model's size and memory footprint, leading to faster inference.

Pruning: Pruning involves removing less important connections in the neural network, reducing the model's size and computational complexity.

Knowledge Distillation: This technique involves training a smaller "student" model to mimic the behavior of a larger "teacher" model, resulting in a more efficient model with comparable performance.

3. Software and Configuration Optimization:

Batch Size: Experiment with different batch sizes to find the optimal balance between performance and memory usage. Larger batch sizes generally lead to faster training but require more memory.

Sequence Length: The maximum sequence length the model can process affects memory usage and processing time. If your application doesn't require very long sequences, reducing the sequence length can improve performance.

Caching: Cache precomputed values, such as attention keys and values, to avoid redundant computations and speed up inference.

Data Loading: Use efficient data loading techniques, such as using PyTorch's `DataLoader` with multiple worker processes, to minimize data loading bottlenecks.

Optimized Libraries: Use optimized libraries and frameworks, such as PyTorch's `torch.compile` (for PyTorch 2.0 and later) or ONNX Runtime, for faster inference.

4. Task-Specific Optimization:

Prompt Engineering: Carefully crafting prompts can significantly impact the model's performance. Experiment with different prompt formats and wording to find what works best for your specific task.

Fine-tuning: Fine-tuning the pre-trained model on a task-specific dataset can significantly improve its performance on that task.

Hyperparameter Tuning: Experiment with different hyperparameters, such as learning rate, batch size, and optimizer settings, to optimize the training process.

5. Monitoring and Profiling:

Profiling Tools: Use profiling tools to identify performance bottlenecks in your code.

Monitoring Metrics: Monitor key metrics, such as GPU utilization, memory usage, and training loss, to track the progress of your training and identify areas for improvement.

By applying these optimization techniques, you can significantly improve the performance of Llama 3.1 for your specific needs, making it more efficient and effective for your applications. Remember to prioritize the optimizations that are most relevant to your use case and hardware constraints.

Chapter 4

Prompt Engineering for Llama 3.1

4.1 Crafting Effective Prompts: Best Practices and Techniques

Prompt engineering is the art of crafting effective instructions or inputs for large language models (LLMs) to elicit desired outputs. A well-crafted prompt can significantly impact the quality and relevance of the generated text. This section will explore best practices and techniques for creating effective prompts for Llama 3.1.

1. Clarity and Specificity:

Be Explicit: Clearly state what you want the model to do. Avoid ambiguity and vague language.

Provide Context: Give the model sufficient context to understand the task. This can include background information, examples, or specific instructions.

Define the Output Format: Specify the desired format of the output, such as a list, a paragraph, a table, or code.

Example:

Poor Prompt: "Write something about cats."

Good Prompt: "Write a short paragraph describing the physical characteristics and common behaviors of domestic cats."

2. Instruction Following:

Use Keywords: Use keywords that indicate the type of task you want the model to perform, such as "summarize," "translate," "explain," "write," "generate," "classify," etc.

Use Imperative Verbs: Use imperative verbs (e.g., "Summarize this text," "Translate this sentence") to give clear instructions.

Example:

Prompt: "Summarize the following article in three bullet points: [article text]"

3. Providing Examples (Few-Shot Learning):

Demonstrate the Desired Output: Providing a few examples of the desired input-output pairs can significantly improve the model's performance, especially for complex tasks. This is known as few-shot learning.

Example:

Prompt:

Translate English to French:

English: Hello, how are you?
French: Bonjour, comment allez-vous ?

English: Thank you very much.
French: Merci beaucoup.

English: Good morning.
French:

4. Using Delimiters:

Separate Instructions and Input: Use delimiters (e.g., triple backticks ```, quotes "", or specific symbols) to clearly separate instructions from the input text. This helps the model understand the different parts of the prompt.

Example:

Prompt: "Summarize the following text: [text]"

5. Controlling the Output Length:

Specify Word Count or Character Limit: You can specify the desired length of the output by providing a word count or character limit.

Use Keywords like "Short" or "Concise": Use keywords like "short," "concise," or "brief" to indicate that you want a shorter output.

Example:

Prompt: "Write a short summary of this book (approximately 100 words): [book description]"

6. Iterative Prompting:

Refine Your Prompts: Don't expect to get the perfect output with the first prompt. Experiment with different phrasing and instructions to refine your prompts and achieve better results.

Provide Feedback: If the model's output is not what you expected, provide feedback by modifying the prompt or giving further instructions.

7. Advanced Prompting Techniques:

Chain-of-Thought Prompting: Encourage the model to explain its reasoning process step by step before providing the final answer. This can improve the accuracy of complex reasoning tasks.

Role-Playing: Instruct the model to adopt a specific persona or role. This can be useful for tasks like creative writing or dialogue generation.

By following these best practices and techniques, you can craft effective prompts that elicit desired outputs from Llama 3.1 and unlock its full potential for a wide range of applications.

4.2   Prompt Engineering Strategies for Different Tasks

Different tasks require different prompting strategies to achieve optimal results. This section will explore specific prompt engineering techniques tailored to common use cases for Llama 3.1.

1. Text Generation (Creative Writing, Storytelling):

Provide a Starting Point: Give the model a starting sentence, a brief description of the setting, or a few keywords to kickstart the creative process.

Specify the Genre or Style: Indicate the desired genre (e.g., science fiction, fantasy, romance) or writing style (e.g., formal, informal, humorous).

Define Characters and Plot Points: If you have specific characters or plot points in mind, include them in the prompt.

Use Open-Ended Prompts: For more creative freedom, use open-ended prompts that encourage the model to explore different possibilities.

Example (Storytelling):

"Write a short story about a robot who discovers a hidden world beneath the ocean."

2. Text Summarization:

Clearly Indicate the Text to Summarize: Use delimiters (e.g., ```) to clearly separate the text to be summarized from the instructions.

Specify the Desired Length: Indicate the desired length of the summary (e.g., "Summarize this in three sentences," "Write a 100-word summary").

Focus on Key Information: Instruct the model to focus on the most important information in the text.

Example (Summarization):

"Summarize the following article in a single paragraph: [article text]"

3. Translation:

Clearly Indicate the Source and Target Languages: Specify the languages you want to translate between (e.g., "Translate English to Spanish").

Provide the Text to Translate: Clearly indicate the text you want to translate.

Example (Translation):

"Translate the following sentence from English to German: 'Hello, how are you?'"

4. Question Answering:

Clearly State the Question: Formulate your question clearly and concisely.

Provide Context if Necessary: If the question requires context, provide relevant background information.

Example (Question Answering):

"What is the capital of France?"

5. Code Generation:

Specify the Programming Language: Clearly indicate the programming language you want the model to use (e.g., "Write a Python function").

Describe the Functionality: Clearly describe what the code should do.

Provide Examples or Input/Output Specifications: Providing examples or input/output specifications can help the model generate more accurate and functional code.

Example (Code Generation):

"Write a Python function that calculates the factorial of a given number."

6. Classification:

Provide Examples of Different Categories: Provide examples of different categories or classes to help the model understand the classification task.

Clearly Indicate the Input to Classify: Clearly indicate the input you want the model to classify.

Example (Classification):

"Classify the following movie review as positive or negative: 'This movie was absolutely amazing! The acting was superb, and the plot was captivating.'"

By tailoring your prompts to the specific task at hand, you can significantly improve the performance of Llama 3.1 and achieve more accurate and relevant results. Remember to experiment with different prompting strategies and iterate on your prompts to find what works best for your specific use case.

4.3 Advanced Prompting Techniques: Few-Shot Learning and Chain-of-Thought

While basic prompting techniques are effective for many tasks, advanced techniques like few-shot learning and chain-of-thought prompting can significantly enhance the performance of Llama 3.1, especially for complex reasoning and problem-solving.

1. Few-Shot Learning:

Few-shot learning involves providing the model with a few examples of input-output pairs to demonstrate the desired behavior. This allows the model to quickly adapt to new tasks without requiring extensive fine-tuning.

How it works: By observing a few examples, the model learns the underlying pattern or relationship between the inputs and outputs. It then uses this learned knowledge to generate outputs for new, unseen inputs.

Benefits:

Reduces the need for large training datasets.

Allows for rapid adaptation to new tasks.

Improves performance on tasks with limited data.

Example (Few-Shot Learning for Sentiment Analysis):

Review: This movie was absolutely fantastic! The acting was superb, and the plot was captivating.
Sentiment: Positive

Review: I was extremely disappointed with this film. The story was boring, and the acting was terrible.
Sentiment: Negative

Review: The food was okay, nothing special. The service was decent.
Sentiment:

In this example, providing two examples of movie reviews with their corresponding sentiment (positive or negative) helps the model understand the task and correctly classify the third review as neutral.

2. Chain-of-Thought Prompting:

Chain-of-thought prompting encourages the model to generate a series of intermediate reasoning steps before providing the final answer. This technique is particularly effective for complex reasoning tasks that require multiple steps of inference.

How it works: By prompting the model to explicitly state its reasoning process, it can better understand the underlying logic of the problem and generate more accurate and reliable solutions.

Benefits:

Improves accuracy on complex reasoning tasks.

Provides insights into the model's decision-making process.

Enhances the model's ability to generalize to new problems.

Example (Chain-of-Thought Prompting for Arithmetic):

Question: Roger has 5 tennis balls. He buys 2 more cans of tennis balls. Each can has 3 tennis balls. How many tennis balls does he have now?

Let's think step by step.

Roger starts with 5 tennis balls.
He buys 2 cans of 3 tennis balls each, which is 2 * 3 = 6 tennis balls.
So, he has a total of 5 + 6 = 11 tennis balls.

Answer: 11

By explicitly prompting the model to "think step by step," it breaks down the problem into smaller, more manageable steps, leading to a correct solution.

Combining Few-Shot Learning and Chain-of-Thought:

These two techniques can be combined to further enhance performance. By providing a few examples of chain-of-thought reasoning, you can guide the model to apply this technique to new problems.

Example (Combining Both):

Question: The cafeteria had 23 apples. If they used 20 to make lunch and bought 6 more, how many apples do they have?

Let's think step by step.
They started with 23 apples.
They used 20, so they have 23 - 20 = 3 apples left.
Then they bought 6 more, so they have 3 + 6 = 9 apples.
Answer: 9

Question: There are 15 trees in the grove. Grove workers will plant trees in rows. If they plant 11 more trees in the first row and 5 trees in the second row, how many trees will there be in the grove?

Let's think step by step.

By providing one example of chain-of-thought reasoning, the model is more likely to apply the same reasoning process to the second question.

By mastering these advanced prompting techniques, you can unlock the full potential of Llama 3.1 and build powerful applications that can solve complex problems and generate more insightful and accurate results.

Chapter 5

Building Text Generation Applications with Llama 3.1

5.1   Generating Creative Content: Stories, Poems, and Scripts

Llama 3.1 excels at generating creative content, including stories, poems, and scripts. This section will explore specific prompting strategies and techniques to maximize its creative potential.

1. Story Generation:

Provide a Premise or Starting Point: Give the model a brief description of the story's setting, characters, or plot. This can be a single sentence, a short paragraph, or a few keywords.

Specify the Genre: Indicate the desired genre, such as science fiction, fantasy, romance, thriller, or horror.

Define Characters: Provide details about the main characters, including their personalities, motivations, and relationships.

Outline Plot Points: If you have specific plot points in mind, include them in the prompt.

Control the Tone and Style: Specify the desired tone (e.g., humorous, serious, suspenseful) and writing style (e.g., descriptive, concise, poetic).

Example (Story Generation):

Write a short science fiction story about a lone astronaut who discovers an alien artifact on Mars. The story should have a suspenseful tone and focus on the astronaut's internal conflict.

2. Poem Generation:

Specify the Form or Style: Indicate the desired poetic form (e.g., sonnet, haiku, free verse) or style (e.g., romantic, melancholic, humorous).

Provide a Theme or Topic: Give the model a theme or topic to focus on.

Use Keywords or Imagery: Include keywords or imagery that you want the poem to evoke.

Control the Length and Structure: Specify the desired length of the poem and any structural requirements (e.g., number of stanzas, rhyme scheme).

Example (Poem Generation):

Write a short free verse poem about the beauty of a winter snowfall. Use imagery of white blankets, silent forests, and frozen streams.

3. Script Generation:

Specify the Format: Indicate the desired script format (e.g., screenplay, stage play, teleplay).

Define Characters and Setting: Provide details about the characters and the setting.

Outline the Plot or Scene: Describe the plot or scene you want the script to depict.

Include Dialogue and Action: Provide examples of dialogue and action to guide the model.

Example (Script Generation):

Write a short scene for a stage play between two characters, a detective and a suspect, in a dimly lit interrogation room. The scene should focus on the detective's attempts to extract a confession from the suspect.

DETECTIVE: (Leans forward) We know you were there that night.
SUSPECT: (Nervously) I told you, I wasn't.

4. Advanced Techniques for Creative Content Generation:

Temperature Control: The "temperature" parameter controls the randomness of the model's output. A lower temperature (e.g., 0.2) results in more deterministic and predictable text, while a higher temperature (e.g., 0.8) results in more creative and surprising text.

Top-p (Nucleus Sampling): This technique selects the next word from a subset of the most likely words, rather than always choosing the most likely word. This can lead to more diverse and interesting outputs.

Iterative Refinement: Generate multiple outputs and then select the best ones. You can then further refine these outputs by providing feedback to the model or editing the text directly.

By using these strategies and experimenting with different prompts and parameters, you can leverage Llama 3.1 to generate a wide range of creative content, from compelling stories and evocative poems to engaging scripts.

5.2 Text Summarization and Paraphrasing

Llama 3.1 is highly capable of summarizing and paraphrasing text. These are crucial NLP tasks with numerous applications, from condensing lengthy articles to simplifying complex information. This section will explore effective prompting strategies for these tasks.

1. Text Summarization:

Summarization aims to create a shorter version of a text while retaining its key information. There are two main types:

Extractive Summarization: Selects important sentences or phrases directly from the original text and combines them to form a summary.

Abstractive Summarization: Generates a summary by understanding the meaning of the text and rephrasing it in a concise way, potentially using new words and phrases. Llama 3.1 primarily performs abstractive summarization.

Prompting Strategies for Summarization:

Clearly Indicate the Text: Use delimiters (e.g., ```, "", or specific symbols) to clearly separate the text to be summarized from the instructions.

Specify the Desired Length: Indicate the desired length of the summary (e.g., "Summarize this in three sentences," "Write a 100-word summary," "Create a bullet-point summary").

Focus on Key Information: Instruct the model to focus on the most important information, main points, or key arguments.

Target a Specific Audience: If the summary is intended for a specific audience, mention it in the prompt (e.g., "Summarize this for a non-technical audience").

Examples:

Short Summary: "Summarize the following article in onesentence: `[article text]`"

Detailed Summary: "Provide a detailed summary of the following research paper, focusing on the methodology and key findings: `[research paper text]`"

Bullet-Point Summary: "Create a bullet-point summary of the following meeting minutes: `[meeting minutes text]`"

2. Paraphrasing:

Paraphrasing involves expressing the meaning of a text using different words and sentence structures while preserving the original meaning.

Prompting Strategies for Paraphrasing:

Clearly Indicate the Text: Use delimiters to clearly separate the text to be paraphrased.

Specify the Desired Style or Tone: You can request a more formal or informal paraphrase.

Avoid Plagiarism: Explicitly instruct the model to avoidplagiarism by using its own words and sentence structures.

Examples:

Simple Paraphrase: "Paraphrase the following sentence: `[sentence]`"

Formal Paraphrase: "Provide a formal paraphrase of the following paragraph: [paragraph]"

Paraphrase for a Specific Audience: "Paraphrase the following technical explanation for a general audience: [technical explanation]"

Emphasis on Avoiding Plagiarism: "Paraphrase the following text in your own words, ensuring that the paraphrase is original and does not plagiarize the source: [text]"

Combining Summarization and Paraphrasing:

Sometimes you might need to both summarize and paraphrase a text. You can combine these instructions in a single prompt.

Example:

"Summarize and paraphrase the following article in two sentences: [article text]"

Key Considerations:

Context Window Limitations: Be mindful of Llama 3.1's context window. If the text is too long, you may need to break it down into smaller chunks and summarize or paraphrase them separately.

Iterative Refinement: If the initial output isn't satisfactory, refine your prompt or provide additional instructions.

Evaluation: Evaluate the quality of the summaries and paraphrases to ensure they are accurate, concise, and coherent.

By using these prompting strategies, you can effectively leverage Llama 3.1 for text summarization and paraphrasing tasks, improving efficiency and understanding of textual information.

5.3 Building Chatbots and Conversational AI

Llama 3.1's ability to understand and generate human language makes it a powerful tool for building chatbots and conversational AI applications. This section explores the techniques and strategies for creating effective conversational agents.

1. Designing the Chatbot's Persona:

Define the Chatbot's Purpose: What is the chatbot designed to do? (e.g., provide customer support, answer questions, offer recommendations, engage in casual conversation).

Create a Personality: Give the chatbot a distinct personality and tone of voice. This can include traits like friendly, professional, humorous, or informative.

Establish a Communication Style: Determine how the chatbot will communicate (e.g., formal or informal language, use of emojis, length of responses).

2. Prompt Engineering for Conversational Flow:

Context Management: Maintain context throughout the conversation by including previous turns in the prompt. This allows the chatbot to remember previous interactions and provide more relevant responses.

Turn-Taking and Dialogue Structure: Structure the prompt to clearly separate user input and chatbot responses.

Handling User Input: Design prompts to handle various types of user input, including questions, statements, commands, and even irrelevant or nonsensical input.

Generating Diverse Responses: Use techniques like temperature control and top-p sampling to encourage the chatbot to generate diverse and engaging responses.

Example (Context Management):

User: Hello, I'd like to order a pizza.
Chatbot: Sure, what kind of pizza would you like?
User: Pepperoni.
Chatbot: Okay, one pepperoni pizza. What size would you like?

In this example, each turn of the conversation is included in the subsequent prompt, allowing the chatbot to maintain context.

3. Implementing Conversational Logic:

Conditional Logic: Use conditional logic (e.g., if-then statements) to guide the conversation based on user input.

State Management: Maintain state variables to track the progress of the conversation and store information provided by the user.

Fallback Mechanisms: Implement fallback mechanisms to handle situations where the chatbot doesn't understand the user's input or cannot provide a relevant response. This could involve asking for clarification or directing the user to a human agent.

4. Advanced Techniques:

Memory and External Knowledge: Integrate external knowledge sources, such as databases or APIs, to provide the chatbot with access to additional information.

Sentiment Analysis: Use sentiment analysis to understand the user's emotional state and tailor the chatbot's responses accordingly.

Entity Recognition: Use entity recognition to identify key information in the user's input, such as dates, locations, or product names.

Reinforcement Learning: Use reinforcement learning techniques to train the chatbot to optimize its conversational strategies and achieve specific goals.

Example (Prompt with Context and Conditional Logic):

Previous turns:
User: Hello, I'd like to order a pizza.
Chatbot: Sure, what kind of pizza would you like?

Current turn:
User: Pepperoni.

Chatbot: Okay, one pepperoni pizza. What size would you like?

If user selects size:
Chatbot: Great! And what is your address for delivery?

If user asks about prices:
Chatbot: Our pepperoni pizzas are \$10 for a small, \$15 for a medium, and \$20 for a large.

5. Tools and Frameworks:

LangChain: A powerful framework that simplifies the development of LLM-powered applications, including chatbots. It provides tools for prompt management, memory management, and integrating with external data sources.

Hugging Face Transformers: Provides pre-trained models and tools for building conversational AI applications.

By using these techniques and tools, you can build sophisticated and engaging chatbots that can effectively interact with users and provide valuable assistance. Remember to focus on creating a natural and human-like conversational experience.

Chapter 6

Fine-Tuning Llama 3.1 for Specific Tasks

6.1 The Importance of Fine-Tuning: Adapting the Model to Your Needs

While pre-trained models like Llama 3.1 possess impressive general-purpose language understanding and generation capabilities, fine-tuning is often crucial for achieving optimal performance on specific tasks or domains. This chapter explores the importance of fine-tuning and how it can significantly enhance the model's effectiveness.

1. What is Fine-Tuning?

Fine-tuning involves taking a pre-trained language model and further training it on a smaller, task-specific dataset. This process adjusts the model's parameters to better align with the characteristics of the target task, leading to improved performance.

2. Why is Fine-Tuning Important?

Improved Accuracy: Fine-tuning allows the model to learn the nuances and specific patterns of the target task, leading to significantly higher accuracy compared to using the pre-trained model directly

Enhanced Performance on Specific Domains: Pre-trained models are trained on a broad range of data, but they may not be optimized for specific domains like medical text, legal documents, or financial reports. Fine-tuning on domain-specific data allows the model to become an expert in that area.

Reduced Prompt Engineering Effort: While prompt engineering is essential, fine-tuning can reduce the reliance on complex prompts by directly adapting the model to the task.

Better Generalization: Fine-tuning can sometimes improve the model's ability to generalize to new, unseen examples within the target domain.

3. When to Fine-Tune:

Specific Tasks: If you have a well-defined task with a sufficient dataset, fine-tuning is highly recommended. Examples include sentiment analysis, text classification, question answering on a specific knowledge base, and generating specific types of text (e.g., product descriptions, code in a particular language).

Domain Adaptation: If your application deals with a specific domain that is not well-represented in the pre-training data, fine-tuning on domain-specific data is crucial.

Performance Bottlenecks: If you are not achieving satisfactory performance with prompt engineering alone, fine-tuning is a good option.

4. When Not to Fine-Tune:

Limited Data: If you have very limited data for your task, fine-tuning may not be effective and could even lead to overfitting. In such cases, few-shot learning with careful prompt engineering might be a better approach.

Simple Tasks: For very simple tasks that can be easily solved with basic prompt engineering, fine-tuning might not be necessary.

Resource Constraints: Fine-tuning can be computationally expensive, especially for large models. If you have limited resources, consider using smaller models or exploring other optimization techniques.

5. Fine-Tuning Process:

The fine-tuning process typically involves the following steps:

Data Preparation: Prepare a dataset of input-output pairs for the target task.

Model Selection: Choose a pre-trained Llama 3.1 model as a starting point.

Hyperparameter Tuning: Select appropriate hyperparameters, such as learning rate, batch size, and number of training epochs.

Training: Train the model on the task-specific dataset.

Evaluation: Evaluate the fine-tuned model's performance on a held-out test set.

6. Techniques for Efficient Fine-Tuning:

Parameter-Efficient Fine-Tuning (PEFT): Methods like LoRA (Low-Rank Adaptation) and prefix-tuning allow you to fine-tune only a small subset of the model's parameters, significantly reducing computational costs and memory requirements.

Quantization: Applying quantization during fine-tuning can also reduce memory usage.

By understanding the importance of fine-tuning and following the appropriate procedures, you can effectively adapt Llama 3.1 to your specific needs and achieve significantly better results in your applications.

6.2 Fine-Tuning Techniques and Best Practices

Fine-tuning is a critical process for adapting pre-trained language models like Llama 3.1 to specific tasks and domains. This section outlines effective techniques and best practices to maximize the benefits of fine-tuning.

1. Data Preparation:

Data Quality: The quality of your training data is paramount. Ensure the data is accurate, relevant, and representative of the target task or domain. Clean and preprocess the data to remove noise and inconsistencies.

Data Quantity: While fine-tuning requires less data than pre-training, having a sufficient amount of data is still important. The exact amount depends on the complexity of the task and the size of the model. Generally, more data leads to better performance.

Data Formatting: Format your data into input-output pairs. The input should be the text or context provided to the model, and the output should be the desired response or label.

Data Splitting: Split your data into training, validation, and test sets. The training set is used to train the model, the validation set is used[1] to monitor performance during training and tune hyperparameters, and the test set is used to evaluate the final model's performance.

2. Model Selection:

Base Model: Choose a pre-trained Llama 3.1 model that is appropriate for your task. Larger models generally have greater capacity but require more resources.

Task Similarity: Select a base model that was pre-trained on data similar to your target domain or task.

3. Hyperparameter Tuning:

Learning Rate: The learning rate controls how quickly the model's parameters are updated during training. Start with a small learning rate (e.g., 1e-5 or 5e-5) and adjust it based on the training progress.

Batch Size: The batch size determines how many examples are processed at once. Larger batch sizes can speed up training but require more memory.

Number of Epochs: The number of epochs determines how many times the model iterates over the training data. Too few epochs may result in underfitting, while too many epochs may result in overfitting.

Optimizer: Use an appropriate optimizer, such as AdamW, which is commonly used for fine-tuning language models.

Learning Rate Scheduler: Use a learning rate scheduler, such as a linear or cosine scheduler, to adjust the learning rate during training.

4. Training Techniques:

Full Fine-Tuning: Updates all the parameters of the pre-trained model. This can be computationally expensive but often yields the best results.

Parameter-Efficient Fine-Tuning (PEFT): Methods like LoRA (Low-Rank Adaptation), prefix-tuning, and adapters fine-tune only a small subset of the model's parameters, significantly reducing computational costs and memory requirements. This is highly recommended for larger models and resource-constrained environments.

Gradient Accumulation: If you have limited GPU memory, you can simulate larger batch sizes by accumulating gradients over multiple smaller batches.

5. Evaluation and Monitoring:

Evaluation Metrics: Use appropriate evaluation metrics for your task. For example, accuracy, precision, recall, and F1-score for classification tasks; BLEU, ROUGE, and METEOR for text generation tasks.

Validation Set Monitoring: Monitor the model's performance on the validation set during training to detect overfitting.

Early Stopping: Stop training if the model's performance on the validation set plateaus or starts to decrease.

6. Best Practices:

Start with a Small Dataset and Iterate: Start with a smaller subset of your data and gradually increase it as needed.

Regularly Evaluate Performance: Evaluate the model's performance on the validation set regularly during training.

Experiment with Different Hyperparameters: Experiment with different hyperparameter values to find the optimal settings for your task.

Use Pre-trained Checkpoints: If you are fine-tuning a large model, consider using pre-trained checkpoints to speed up the training process.

Use Tools and Libraries: Leverage tools and libraries like the Hugging Face Transformers library and PEFT libraries to simplify the fine-tuning process.

By following these techniques and best practices, you can effectively fine-tune Llama 3.1 for your specific needs and achieve optimal performance. Remember to carefully monitor the training process and evaluate the model's performance to ensure you are achieving the desired results.

6.3 Evaluating Fine-Tuned Models: Metrics and Methods

After fine-tuning Llama 3.1, it's crucial to evaluate its performance to ensure it meets your requirements. This section outlines common metrics and methods used to assess the quality of fine-tuned language models.

1. General Evaluation Principles:

Held-Out Test Set: Always evaluate your model on a held-out test set that was not used during training or validation. This provides an unbiased estimate of the model's performance on unseen data.

Appropriate Metrics: Choose evaluation metrics that are relevant to your specific task.

Human Evaluation: For some tasks, especially those involving subjective qualities like creativity or fluency, human evaluation can be valuable.

2. Metrics for Classification Tasks:

Accuracy: The percentage of correctly classified instances.

Precision: The proportion of true positives among the instances predicted as positive.

Recall: The proportion of true positives among the actual positive instances.

F1-Score: The harmonic mean of precision and recall, providing a balanced measure of performance.

Confusion Matrix: A table that summarizes the model's classification performance by showing the number of true positives, true negatives, false positives, and false negatives.

3. Metrics for Text Generation Tasks:

Evaluating text generation is more complex than classification due to the open-ended nature of the task.

BLEU (Bilingual Evaluation Understudy): Measures the overlap of n-grams (sequences of n words) between the generated text and one or more reference texts.

ROUGE (Recall-Oriented Understudy for Gisting Evaluation): Measures the overlap of n-grams, word sequences, and word pairs between the generated text and reference texts, focusing on recall.

METEOR (Metric for Evaluation of Translation with Explicit Ordering): Considers synonyms and paraphrases, addressing some of the limitations of BLEU.

BERTScore: Uses contextual embeddings from BERT to measure semantic similarity between the generated text and reference texts.

Perplexity: Measures how well the model predicts the next word in a sequence. Lower perplexity indicates better performance. However, perplexity doesn't directly measure the quality of generated text in terms of coherence or relevance.

4. Metrics for Question Answering:

Exact Match (EM): Measures the percentage of generated answers that exactly match the reference answer.

F1-Score: Measures the overlap of words between the generated answer and the reference answer, similar to text generation but often calculated at the word level.

5. Methods for Evaluation:

Automatic Evaluation: Using metrics like BLEU, ROUGE, and BERTScore to automatically compare the generated text to reference texts. This is efficient but may not capture all aspects of text quality.

Human Evaluation: Asking human evaluators to rate the quality of the generated text based on criteria like fluency, coherence, relevance, and accuracy. This is more time-consuming and expensive but can provide valuable insights.

A/B Testing: Comparing different versions of the model or different prompting strategies by showing their outputs to human users and asking for their preferences.

6. Considerations for Choosing Metrics:

Task-Specific Requirements: Choose metrics that are relevant to the specific requirements of your task. For example, if recall is more important than precision, prioritize ROUGE over BLEU.

Correlation with Human Judgments: Choose metrics that correlate well with human judgments of text quality.

Limitations of Automatic Metrics: Be aware of the limitations of automatic metrics and consider using human evaluation to supplement them.

Example:

If you are fine-tuning Llama 3.1 for a text summarization task, you might use ROUGE-L (which measures the longest common subsequence) as a primary metric, supplemented by human evaluation to assess the coherence and readability of the summaries.

By using appropriate metrics and methods, you can effectively evaluate the performance of your fine-tuned Llama 3.1 models and ensure they meet your application's requirements. Remember to consider the limitations of automatic metrics and incorporate human evaluation where necessary.

Chapter 7

Building Applications with Llama 3.1 APIs and Integrations

7.1 Leveraging Llama 3.1 APIs for Seamless Integration

It appears you might be referring to running Llama 2 as an API, as there's no publicly available API directly from Meta for Llama models. However, there are several ways to achieve similar functionality. Here's a breakdown of how to leverage Llama 2 for seamless integration into your applications:

1. Using Third-Party APIs:

Providers like Replicate, Together AI, and others: These platforms offer APIs that host Llama 2 and other large language models, allowing you to easily integrate them into your applications with simple API calls.[1]

Benefits:

Easy to use and integrate.

Handles infrastructure and scaling for you.

Often provides features like rate limiting and monitoring.

Considerations:

Cost: These services typically charge based on usage.

Data privacy: Ensure the provider has appropriate data privacy policies.

Customization: Limited control over model fine-tuning or customization.

2. Deploying Llama 2 on Your Own Infrastructure:

Using tools like Hugging Face Transformers and `text-generation-inference`: You can deploy Llama 2 on your own servers or cloud instances using these tools.[2]

Benefits:

Full control over the model and its configuration.

Greater flexibility for customization and fine-tuning.

Potentially lower cost for high-volume usage.

Considerations:

Requires technical expertise to set up and maintain the infrastructure.

Responsible for scaling and ensuring reliability.

Higher upfront investment in hardware or cloud resources.

3. Key API Functionalities (Regardless of Deployment Method):

Text Generation: The core functionality is generating text based on a given prompt. This typically involves sending a request with the prompt and receiving a response with the generated text.

Prompt Engineering: You can use various prompt engineering techniques, such as few-shot learning and chain-of-thought prompting, to guide the model's output.[3]

Parameter Control: You can usually control parameters like temperature (for controlling randomness), `max_new_tokens` (for limiting the length of the generated text), and top-p (for nucleus sampling).

4. Example API Interaction (Conceptual):

Python
```
import requests

API_URL = "https://api.example-llama-provider.com/generate"  # Replace with actual API URL
API_KEY = "YOUR_API_KEY"

prompt = "Write a short story about a cat who goes on an adventure."

headers = {
    "Authorization": f"Bearer {API_KEY}",
    "Content-Type": "application/json",
}

data = {
    "prompt": prompt,
    "max_new_tokens": 200,
    "temperature": 0.7,
}

response = requests.post(API_URL, headers=headers, json=data)

if response.status_code == 200:
    generated_text = response.json()["generated_text"]
```

```
    print(generated_text)
else:
    print(f"Error: {response.status_code}")
    print(response.text)
```

5. Choosing the Right Approach:

For quick prototyping and small-scale applications: Using a third-party API is often the easiest and most cost-effective option.

For large-scale applications, fine-tuning, or strict data privacy requirements: Deploying Llama 2 on your own infrastructure provides greater control and flexibility.

By understanding these different approaches, you can effectively leverage Llama 2's powerful language generation capabilities and integrate them seamlessly into your applications.

7.2 Integrating Llama 3.1 with Other AI Tools and Platforms

Integrating Llama 3.1 with other AI tools and platforms can significantly enhance its capabilities and enable you to build more sophisticated and powerful applications. Here are some key integration strategies:

1. Vector Databases (for Knowledge Retrieval):

How it works: Vector databases like Pinecone, Weaviate, and Milvus store data as vector embeddings, which are numerical representations of the data's meaning. You can use Llama 3.1 to generate embeddings for your data and store them in the vector database. Then, when a user asks a question, you can use the vector database to retrieve relevant information and provide it as context to Llama 3.1. This is known as Retrieval Augmented Generation (RAG).

Benefits:

Provides Llama 3.1 with access to external knowledge sources.

Improves accuracy and relevance of responses.

Allows for handling of large amounts of information that cannot fit within the model's context window.

2. Other NLP Tools:

Tokenizers: Use specialized tokenizers like SentencePiece or tiktoken for efficient text preprocessing.

Sentiment Analysis Tools: Integrate sentiment analysis models to understand the user's emotional state and tailor Llama 3.1's responses accordingly.

Named Entity Recognition (NER) Tools: Use NER tools to identify key information in the user's input, such as dates, locations, or product names.

3. Development Frameworks:

LangChain: A powerful framework that simplifies the development of LLM-powered applications. It provides tools for prompt management, memory management, and integrating with external data sources and other tools.

Hugging Face Transformers: Provides pre-trained models, tokenizers, and other tools for working with Llama 3.1 and other language models.

4. Cloud Platforms:

Cloud-based AI Services: Integrate Llama 3.1 with cloud-based AI services like Google Cloud AI Platform, AWS SageMaker, or Azure Machine Learning for model deployment, scaling, and management.

Serverless Functions: Use serverless functions to create scalable and cost-effective APIs for accessing Llama 3.1's capabilities.

5. Example Integration with a Vector Database (Conceptual):

Embed Data: Use Llama 3.1 (or another embedding model) to generate vector embeddings for your knowledge base (e.g., a collection of documents).

Store Embeddings: Store the embeddings in a vector database.

User Query: Receive a user query.

Generate Embedding: Use Llama 3.1 to generate an embedding for the user query.

Retrieve Relevant Information: Query the vector database to retrieve the most similar embeddings (i.e., the most relevant information).

Provide Context to Llama 3.1: Combine the retrieved information with the user query to create a prompt for Llama 3.1.

Generate Response: Use Llama 3.1 to generate a response based on the provided context.

6. Benefits of Integration:

Enhanced Capabilities: Combining Llama 3.1 with other tools can significantly enhance its capabilities and enable it to perform more complex tasks.

Improved Accuracy and Relevance: Integrating with knowledge retrieval systems can improve the accuracy and relevance of Llama 3.1's responses.

Increased Efficiency: Using specialized tools for specific tasks can improve overall efficiency.

Greater Flexibility: Integrating with different platforms and services provides greater flexibility in building and deploying applications.

By strategically integrating Llama 3.1 with other AI tools and platforms, you can create powerful and versatile applications that leverage the strengths of each component.

7.3 Building Scalable and Production-Ready Applications with Llama 3.1

Taking a prototype Llama 3.1 application to a production-ready system requires careful consideration of scalability, reliability, and maintainability. This section outlines key strategies for building robust and scalable applications.

1. Infrastructure Considerations:

Cloud Deployment: Cloud platforms like AWS, Google Cloud, and Azure offer scalable and reliable infrastructure for deploying Llama 3.1 applications. They provide services like virtual machines, containers, and serverless functions that can be easily scaled to handle increasing traffic.

Containerization (Docker, Kubernetes): Using containers allows you to package your application and its dependencies into a single unit, making it easier to deploy and manage across different environments. Kubernetes can be used to orchestrate and scale containerized applications.

Load Balancing: Distribute traffic across multiple instances of your application to prevent overload and ensure high availability.

Monitoring and Logging: Implement robust monitoring and logging to track the performance of your application and identify any issues.

2. Model Optimization for Production:

Quantization: Use quantization techniques (e.g., 8-bit quantization) to reduce the model's size and memory footprint, leading to faster inference and lower resource consumption.

Model Pruning: Remove less important connections in the neural network to reduce the model's complexity and improve efficiency.

Knowledge Distillation: Train a smaller, more efficient model to mimic the behavior of the larger Llama 3.1 model.

Caching: Implement caching mechanisms to store frequently accessed data and reduce the number of requests to the model.

3. API Design and Implementation:

RESTful APIs: Design RESTful APIs for accessing Llama 3.1's capabilities. This allows for easy integration with other applications and services.

Asynchronous Processing: Use asynchronous processing to handle long-running requests and prevent blocking the main thread.

Rate Limiting: Implement rate limiting to prevent abuse and ensure fair usage of your application.

Authentication and Authorization: Implement appropriate authentication and authorization mechanisms to secure your API.

4. Data Management:

Efficient Data Storage: Use efficient data storage solutions, such as databases or cloud storage, to store and manage your data.

Data Preprocessing Pipeline: Implement a robust data preprocessing pipeline to clean, transform, and prepare data for use with Llama 3.1.

5. Monitoring and Maintenance:

Performance Monitoring: Continuously monitor theperformance of your application, including metrics like latency, throughput, and error rates.

Logging and Error Tracking: Implement comprehensive logging and error tracking to identify and resolve any issues.

Model Updates and Maintenance: Establish a process for updating the Llama 3.1 model and retraining it with new data.

6. Example Deployment Architecture (Conceptual):

Load Balancer: Distributes traffic across multiple API servers.

API Servers (Containerized): Run containerized instances of your Llama 3.1 API.

Llama 3.1 Model (Optimized): Deployed on GPUs or CPUs depending on resource availability.

Vector Database (Optional): Stores embeddings for knowledge retrieval.

Database: Stores application data and user information.

Monitoring and Logging System: Collects logs and metrics for monitoring and analysis.

7. Key Considerations for Scalability:

Horizontal Scaling: Scale your application by adding more instances of your API servers.

Auto-Scaling: Use auto-scaling to automatically adjust the number of instances based on traffic demand.

Stateless Architecture: Design your application with a stateless architecture to facilitate horizontal scaling.

By following these strategies, you can build scalable, reliable, and maintainable applications that leverage the power of Llama 3.1 in a production environment. Remember to prioritize performance optimization, robust infrastructure, and thorough monitoring to ensure the success of your application.

Chapter 8

Ethical Considerations and Responsible Use of Llama 3.1

8.1 Addressing Bias and Fairness in Language Models

Large language models (LLMs) like Llama 3.1, trained on massive datasets of text and code, can inadvertently learn and perpetuate biases present in that data. Addressing bias and promoting fairness is crucial for responsible AI development. This section explores the challenges of bias in LLMs and strategies for mitigation.

1. Sources of Bias:

Training Data Bias: The most significant source of bias comes from the training data itself. If the data contains skewed representations of certain groups (e.g., based on gender, race, religion, or socioeconomic status), the model will likely learn these biases.

Data Collection Methods: How data is collected can also introduce bias. For example, if data is collected primarily from online sources, it may overrepresent certain demographics and underrepresent others.

Algorithmic Bias: Even with unbiased data, the model's architecture and training algorithms can introduce bias.

2. Types of Bias:

Representation Bias: Certain groups are underrepresented or overrepresented in the training data, leading to skewed representations in the model.

Stereotyping Bias: The model reinforces harmful stereotypes about certain groups.

Bias in Language Use: The model may exhibit bias in its use of language, such as using different pronouns or adjectives when referring to different groups.

Output Bias: The model's outputs may perpetuate biased or unfair outcomes.

3. Identifying Bias:

Bias Audits: Conduct regular bias audits to assess the model's performance across different demographic groups.

Targeted Testing: Test the model on specific examples designed to reveal potential biases.

Benchmark Datasets: Use benchmark datasets designed to evaluate bias in language models.

Qualitative Analysis: Analyze the model's outputs qualitatively to identify any patterns of bias.

4. Mitigation Strategies:

Data Balancing: Balance the training data to ensure that all groups are adequately represented.

Data Augmentation: Augment the data with examples that challenge existing biases.

Bias Detection and Removal During Training: Use techniques to detect and remove bias during the training process.

Adversarial Training: Train the model to be robust against adversarial examples that are designed to exploit biases.

Prompt Engineering: Carefully craft prompts to avoid triggering biases.

Model Calibration: Calibrate the model's outputs to ensure they are fair across different groups.

Transparency and Explainability: Make the model's decision-making process more transparent and explainable.

Human Oversight: Incorporate human oversight in the development and deployment of LLMs.

5. Ethical Considerations:

Fairness and Equity: Strive for fairness and equity in the model's outputs and outcomes.

Accountability and Responsibility: Establish clear lines of accountability and responsibility for addressing bias in LLMs.

Societal Impact: Consider the potential societal impact of LLMs and take steps to mitigate any negative consequences.

Example of Bias Mitigation through Prompt Engineering:

Instead of a potentially biased prompt like: "Write a story about a successful doctor," which might implicitly assume a male doctor, use a more neutral prompt like: "Write a story about a successful medical professional."

Addressing bias in LLMs is an ongoing challenge, but by using these strategies and remaining vigilant, we can work towards developing more fair and equitable AI systems. It's important to remember that technical solutions alone are not sufficient; addressing bias also requires careful consideration of ethical and societal implications.

8.2 Mitigating the Risks of Misinformation and Misuse of Llama 3.1

The powerful capabilities of large language models like Llama 3.1 also raise concerns about their potential for misuse, particularly in generating and spreading misinformation.[1] This section focuses on strategies to mitigate these risks.

1. Understanding the Risks:

Generation of Misinformation: LLMs can generate realistic and convincing fake news, propaganda, and other forms of misinformation.[2]

Impersonation and Phishing: LLMs can be used to create convincing impersonations of individuals or organizations for phishing attacks or other malicious purposes.[3]

Automated Content Creation for Malicious Purposes: LLMs can be used to automatically generate large volumes of spam, malicious code, or other harmful content.[4]

Bias Amplification: Existing biases in training data can be amplified by LLMs, leading to the spread of harmful stereotypes and discrimination.[5]

2. Mitigation Strategies:

Watermarking and Provenance Tracking: Implement techniques to watermark generated text, making it possible to trace its origin and identify potentially manipulated content.[6]

Content Filtering and Detection: Develop robust content filtering and detection systems to identify and flag potentially harmful or misleading content generated by LLMs.

Prompt Engineering and Input Validation: Carefully design prompts to avoid triggering the generation of harmful content. Implement input validation to prevent malicious or abusive inputs.

Model Calibration and Output Control: Calibrate the model's outputs to reduce the likelihood of generating harmful content. Implement mechanisms to control the style, tone, and content of generated text.

Fine-Tuning for Safety: Fine-tune models on datasets that promote safety and factual accuracy.

Human Oversight and Review: Incorporate human oversight in the development and deployment of LLMs, especially for high-risk applications.[7]

Transparency and Explainability: Make the model's decision-making process more transparent and explainable to facilitate detection of potential misuse.

Responsible Use Guidelines and Policies: Develop clear guidelines and policies for the responsible use of LLMs.

Collaboration and Information Sharing: Foster collaboration and information sharing among researchers, developers, and policymakers to address the challenges of misinformation and misuse.

3. Specific Examples of Mitigation Techniques:

Detecting AI-Generated Text: Develop methods to distinguish between human-written and AI-generated text. This is an active area of research.

Fact-Checking Integration: Integrate LLMs with fact-checking databases and APIs to verify the accuracy of generated information.

Red Teaming: Conduct red teaming exercises to identify potential vulnerabilities and weaknesses in LLM systems.[8]

4. Community and Industry Efforts:

Partnerships and Collaborations: Collaboration between academia, industry, and government is crucial for addressing the challenges of misinformation and misuse.

Standards and Best Practices: Developing industry standards and best practices for the responsible development and deployment of LLMs.

5. User Education and Awareness:

Promoting Critical Thinking: Educating users about the potential for misinformation and promoting critical thinking skills.

Labeling AI-Generated Content: Clearly labeling content generated by AI to help users distinguish it from human-created content.[9]

Mitigating the risks of misinformation and misuse is a complex and ongoing challenge. A multi-faceted approach involving technical solutions, policy development, and user education is essential for ensuring the responsible and beneficial use of Llama 3.1 and other large language models.[10]

8.3 Promoting Responsible AI Development and Deployment of Llama 3.1

Responsible AI development and deployment are paramount, especially with powerful models like Llama 3.1. This section outlines key principles and practices to ensure these models are used ethically and for the benefit of society.

1. Key Principles of Responsible AI:

Fairness and Non-discrimination: AI systems should not perpetuate or amplify biases that discriminate against individuals or groups based on protected characteristics like race, gender, religion, or sexual orientation.

Transparency and Explainability: The decision-making processes of AI systems should be transparent and understandable, allowing for scrutiny and accountability.

Accountability and Responsibility: Clear lines of responsibility and accountability should be established for the development, deployment, and use of AI systems.

Privacy and Data Security: AI systems should respect user privacy and protect sensitive data.

Safety and Reliability: AI systems should be designed and deployed to be safe and reliable, minimizing the risk of harm or unintended consequences.

Human Control and Oversight: Humans should maintain control and oversight over critical decisions made by AI systems.

Societal Benefit: AI systems should be developed and deployed in a way that benefits society as a whole.

2. Practices for Responsible Development and Deployment:

Bias Mitigation: Implement strategies to identify and mitigate bias in training data and models, as discussed in the previous section.

Data Governance: Establish clear data governance policies and procedures to ensure data quality, privacy, and security.

Model Evaluation and Auditing: Regularly evaluate and audit models for bias, fairness, and other ethical considerations.

Explainable AI (XAI): Use XAI techniques to make the model's decision-making process more transparent and understandable.

Human-in-the-Loop Systems: Design systems that incorporate human input and oversight, especially for critical decisions.

Impact Assessments: Conduct impact assessments to evaluate the potential social, economic, and ethical implications of deploying AI systems.

Ethical Guidelines and Frameworks: Adhere to established ethical guidelines and frameworks for AI development and deployment.

Stakeholder Engagement: Engage with stakeholders, including users, experts, and the public, to gather feedback and address concerns.

3. Specific Considerations for Llama 3.1:

Open-Source Nature: While the open-source nature of Llama 3.1 promotes transparency and collaboration, it also means that the model can be used by anyone, including those with malicious intent. Therefore, it's crucial to promote responsible use guidelines and encourage community involvement in addressing potential risks.

Potential for Misinformation: Given its powerful language generation capabilities, Llama 3.1 has the potential to be used for generating misinformation. It's important to implement mitigation strategies, as discussed in the previous section, and educate users about the potential for AI-generated content.

4. Promoting a Culture of Responsible AI:

Education and Training: Provide education and training on responsible AI principles and practices to developers, users, and the public.

Community Building: Foster a community of researchers, developers, and policymakers who are committed to responsible AI.

Open Dialogue and Collaboration: Encourage open dialogue and collaboration on ethical issues related to AI.

5. Examples of Responsible Deployment:

Using Llama 3.1 to create educational resources and tools.

Developing AI-powered accessibility tools for people with disabilities.

Using Llama 3.1 to improve customer service and support.

Developing AI systems for scientific research and discovery.

By adhering to these principles and practices, we can promote the responsible development and deployment of Llama 3.1 and other large language models, ensuring that they are used for the benefit of society while mitigating potential risks. Continuous vigilance, open dialogue, and community involvement are essential for navigating the ethical complexities of AI.

Chapter 9

Advanced Applications and Use Cases of Llama 3.1

9.1 Building AI-Powered Search Engines and Information Retrieval Systems with Llama 3.1

Llama 3.1, with its strong language understanding and generation capabilities, can play a significant role in building advanced search engines and information retrieval systems. This section explores how to leverage Llama 3.1 for this purpose.

1. Traditional Search vs. AI-Powered Search:

Traditional search engines rely on keyword matching and indexing. AI-powered search goes beyond this by understanding the meaning and context of queries and documents, leading to more relevant and accurate results.

2. Key Components of an AI-Powered Search System:

Query Understanding: Processing and understanding the user's search query, including intent recognition, entity recognition, and query expansion.

Document Indexing: Creating a searchable index of documents, often using vector embeddings to represent the semantic meaning of the documents.

Relevance Ranking: Ranking documents based on their relevance to the user's query.

Response Generation: Generating concise and informative summaries or answers to the user's query.

3. Leveraging Llama 3.1 for Search:

Query Understanding: Llama 3.1 can be used to understand the user's search intent, identify key entities in the query, and expand the query with related terms.

Document Embedding: Llama 3.1 can generate vector embeddings for documents, capturing their semantic meaning. These embeddings can be stored in a vector database for efficient similarity search.

Relevance Ranking: By comparing the embedding of the user's query to the embeddings of the documents, you can rank documents based on their semantic similarity.

Answer Generation and Summarization: Llama 3.1 can generate concise answers or summaries of relevant documents, providing users with quick and informative responses.

4. Implementing a Search System with Llama 3.1:

Data Preparation: Collect and preprocess the documents you want to index.

Document Embedding: Use Llama 3.1 (or a dedicated embedding model) to generate vector embeddings for each document.

Vector Database: Store the document embeddings in a vector database (e.g., Pinecone, Weaviate, Milvus).

Query Processing: When a user submits a query:

Use Llama 3.1 to understand the query and generate an embedding.

Query the vector database to retrieve the most similar document embeddings.

Relevance Ranking and Retrieval: Rank the retrieved documents based on their similarity scores.

Answer Generation (Optional): Use Llama 3.1 to generate a concise answer or summary based on the most relevant documents.

Display Results: Display the ranked documents and/or generated answers to the user.

5. Example Workflow (Conceptual):

User Query: "Best restaurants in San Francisco with outdoor seating."

Query Understanding (Llama 3.1): Identifies key entities ("restaurants," "San Francisco," "outdoor seating") and infers the user's intent to find restaurants.

Vector Database Query: Queries the vector database to retrieve documents (e.g., restaurant reviews, websites) with embeddings similar to the query embedding.

Relevance Ranking: Ranks the retrieved documents based on similarity scores.

Answer Generation (Llama 3.1): Generates a concise answer like: "Here are some top-rated restaurants in San Francisco with outdoor seating: [list of restaurants with summaries]."

6. Advantages of Using Llama 3.1 for Search:

Semantic Search: Enables search based on the meaning of queries and documents, rather than just keyword matching.

Contextual Understanding: Captures the context of queries and documents, leading to more relevant results.

Answer Generation: Provides concise and informative answers directly to the user.

Improved User Experience: Offers a more intuitive and efficient search experience.

By combining Llama 3.1 with vector databases and other NLP tools, you can build powerful AI-powered search engines and information retrieval systems that provide users with more relevant, accurate, and informative results.

9.2 Developing Code Generation and Debugging Tools with Llama 3.1

Llama 3.1's ability to understand and generate code makes it a powerful tool for developing code generation and debugging tools. This section explores how to leverage Llama 3.1 for these purposes.

1. Code Generation:

Prompt Engineering for Code Generation:

Specify the Programming Language: Clearly indicate the target programming language (e.g., Python, JavaScript, C++).

Describe the Functionality: Clearly describe what the code should do. Provide detailed specifications, including input and output formats, edge cases, and error handling.

Provide Examples or Test Cases: Providing examples of input-output pairs or test cases can significantly improve the quality and accuracy of the generated code.

Use Natural Language Descriptions: Describe the desired functionality in clear, natural language.

Use Code Comments: Include code comments in the prompt to provide additional context and guidance.

Example (Code Generation):

Write a Python function that takes a list of integers as input and returns the largest number in the list. Include error handling for empty lists.

```
# Example usage:
# input: [1, 5, 2, 8, 3]
# output: 8

# input: []
# output: "Error: Input list is empty."
```

Generating Different Types of Code: Llama 3.1 can be used to generate various types of code, including:
Functions and methods
Classes and objects
Unit tests
Regular expressions
SQL queries
Web page templates (HTML, CSS, JavaScript)

2. Code Debugging:

Identifying Bugs: Llama 3.1 can be used to analyze code and identify potential bugs or errors. You can provide the code and a description of the error or unexpected behavior, and Llama 3.1 can attempt to identify the cause of the problem.

Suggesting Fixes: Based on its analysis, Llama 3.1 can suggest fixes or improvements to the code.

Explaining Code: Llama 3.1 can explain the functionality of a given piece of code in natural language, which can be helpful for understanding complex codebases or for code reviews.

Example (Code Debugging):

Code:
```
def divide(a, b):
  return a / b

result = divide(10, 0)
print(result)
```

Error: ZeroDivisionError: division by zero

Explain the error and suggest a fix.

Llama 3.1 could respond with:

"The error is a ZeroDivisionError, which occurs when you try to divide a number by zero. The fix is to add a check to ensure that the divisor (b) is not zero before performing the division. Here's the corrected code:

Python
```
def divide(a, b):
  if b == 0:
    return "Error: Cannot divide by zero."
  else:
    return a / b

result = divide(10, 0)
print(result) # Output: Error: Cannot divide by zero.
result = divide(10, 2)
print(result) # Output: 5.0
```

` ` ` "

3. Building Code Generation and Debugging Tools:

*   **Integration with IDEs:** Integrate Llama 3.1 into Integrated Development Environments (IDEs) to provide real-time code suggestions, error detection, and debugging assistance.
*   **Command-Line Tools:** Develop command-line tools for generating code or debugging code from the terminal.
*   **Web Applications:** Create web applications that allow users to generate or debug code through a web interface.

4. Key Considerations:

*   **Code Correctness:** While Llama 3.1 can generate plausible code, it's essential to thoroughly test the generated code to ensure its correctness and functionality.
*   **Security:** Be mindful of security risks when generating code, especially when generating code that interacts with external systems or handles sensitive data.
*   **Context Window Limitations:** For very large codebases, you may need to break the code into smaller chunks and process them separately.

By leveraging Llama 3.1's code understanding and generation capabilities, you can build powerful tools that significantly improve developer productivity and code quality. However, human oversight and thorough testing remain crucial for ensuring the reliability and security of generated code.

9.3 Creating Multilingual Applications with Llama 3.1

Llama 3.1's ability to understand and generate text in multiple languages makes it a valuable tool for building multilingual applications. This section explores strategies for leveraging Llama 3.1 for this purpose.

1. Multilingual Capabilities of Llama 3.1:

Llama 3.1 is trained on a massive dataset that includes text in various languages. This allows it to:

Understand and generate text in multiple languages: Llama 3.1 can process and generate text in a wide range of languages, although performance may vary depending on the language and the amount of training data available for that language.

Perform cross-lingual transfer learning: Knowledge learned in one language can be transferred to other languages, improving performance even for languages with limited training data.

Facilitate machine translation: Llama 3.1 can be used for machine translation tasks, translating text from one language to another.

2. Strategies for Building Multilingual Applications:

Prompt Engineering for Translation:

Specify Source and Target Languages: Clearly indicate the source and target languages in the prompt (e.g., "Translate from English to French:").

Provide Context: Providing context can improve the accuracy of translations, especially for ambiguous words or phrases.

Example (Translation):

Translate from English to Spanish: "The quick brown fox jumps over the lazy dog."

Fine-tuning for Specific Languages or Domains: Fine-tuning Llama 3.1 on a dataset of parallel text (text in two or more languages) can significantly improve its performance on specific translation tasks or for specific language pairs.

Multilingual Prompting: You can use prompts that contain text in multiple languages to guide the model's behavior. This can be useful for tasks like cross-lingual information retrieval or code-switching.

Combining with External Translation APIs: For very high-quality translation or for languages with limited support in Llama 3.1, you can combine it with external translation APIs like Google Translate or DeepL. You could use Llama to understand the context and intent of a request and then use a dedicated translation API to perform the translation.

3. Example Application: Multilingual Chatbot:

A multilingual chatbot can be built by combining Llama 3.1 with language detection and translation capabilities.

Language Detection: Detect the language of the user's input.

Translation (If Necessary): If the user's input is not in the chatbot's primary language, translate it to the primary language using Llama 3.1 or an external translation API.

Chatbot Response (Llama 3.1): Use Llama 3.1 to generate a response in the primary language.

Translation (If Necessary): Translate the chatbot's response back to the user's original language.

4. Challenges and Considerations:

Data Availability: The performance of Llama 3.1 on different languages depends on the amount of training data available for those languages. Performance may be lower for low-resource languages.

Cultural Nuances: Language is closely tied to culture, and it's important to be mindful of cultural nuances when building multilingual applications.

Evaluation: Evaluating the quality of multilingual outputs can be challenging. It's important to use appropriate evaluation metrics and consider human evaluation.

5. Benefits of Multilingual Applications:

Increased Accessibility: Makes applications accessible to a wider audience.

Improved User Experience: Provides a more personalized and natural user experience for users who speak different languages.

Global Reach: Enables businesses and organizations to reach a global audience.

By leveraging Llama 3.1's multilingual capabilities and using appropriate strategies, you can build powerful multilingual applications that cater to a diverse user base.

Chapter 10

The Future of Llama and the Evolution of LLMs

10.1 The Roadmap for Llama and Future Developments

While Meta hasn't publicly released a detailed roadmap for Llama 3.1 or future versions, we can discuss likely directions based on current trends in large language model development and Meta's research.

Likely Future Developments for Llama Models:

Increased Model Size and Capacity: A general trend in LLMs is to increase model size (number of parameters) and training data. This often leads to improved performance on various tasks. We can expect future Llama models to follow this trend, potentially with even larger context windows and enhanced capabilities.

Improved Training Efficiency: Training large language models is computationally expensive. Research is ongoing to develop more efficient training methods, which could lead to faster training times and reduced resource requirements for future Llama models.

Enhanced Multilingual Capabilities: While Llama 3.1 already supports multiple languages, future versions may be trained on even larger and more diverse multilingual datasets, leading to improved performance across a wider range of languages, including low-resource languages.

Multimodal Learning: Integrating language models with other modalities, such as images, audio, and video, is an active area of research. Future Llama models may incorporate multimodal learning, allowing them to understand and generate content across different modalities.

Improved Reasoning and Problem-Solving: Research is ongoing to improve the reasoning and problem-solving abilities of LLMs. Future Llama models may incorporate techniques like chain-of-thought prompting and other advanced reasoning methods to tackle more complex tasks.

Increased Focus on Safety and Ethics: As the capabilities of LLMs increase, so do the concerns about their potential misuse. We can expect future Llama models to incorporate improved safety mechanisms and address ethical considerations more thoroughly.

Specialized Models and Fine-tuning Techniques: We may see the development of more specialized Llama models that are fine-tuned for specific tasks or domains, such as code generation, medical text analysis, or legal document processing. Additionally, research on more efficient fine-tuning techniques, like parameter-efficient fine-tuning (PEFT), will likely continue.

Integration with Other Tools and Platforms: Future Llama models will likely be further integrated with other AI tools and platforms, such as vector databases, knowledge graphs, and cloud-based AI services, to enable more powerful and versatile applications.

The Open-Source Nature and Community Involvement:

The open-source nature of Llama models is a key factor in their development. The open-source community plays a vital role in:

Identifying and fixing bugs: The community can help identify and fix bugs in the model and its associated tools.

Developing new features and applications: The community can contribute to the development of new features, tools, and applications that leverage Llama models.

Addressing ethical concerns: The community can contribute to the discussion and development of strategies for addressing ethical concerns related to LLMs.

Overall Direction:

The future of Llama and LLMs in general is likely to be characterized by:

Continued scaling and improvement in performance.

Increased focus on efficiency and accessibility.

Greater emphasis on safety, ethics, and responsible use.

Stronger integration with other AI tools and platforms.

Active community involvement and collaboration.

While a precise roadmap is not publicly available, these trends provide a general direction for the future development of Llama models and their impact on the field of AI.

10.2 Emerging Trends in Large Language Models (LLMs)

The field of Large Language Models is rapidly evolving, with new research and developments constantly emerging. Here are some of the key trends shaping the future of LLMs:

1. Multimodality:

Integrating with other modalities: Moving beyond text, LLMs are increasingly being integrated with other data modalities like images, audio, video, and even sensor data. This allows for more comprehensive understanding of the world and the creation of more versatile AI systems.

Examples: Models that can generate image captions, create videos from text descriptions, or understand and respond to spoken language.

2. Efficiency and Accessibility:

Parameter-Efficient Fine-Tuning (PEFT): Techniques like LoRA, adapters, and prefix-tuning allow for efficient fine-tuning of large models using significantly fewer resources. This makes fine-tuning more accessible to researchers and developers with limited computational resources.

Quantization and Pruning: These techniques reduce the size and computational complexity of models, making them easier to deploy on resource-constrained devices like mobile phones and edge devices.

Specialized Hardware: The development of specialized hardware, such as new generations of GPUs and TPUs, is driving further improvements in training and inference efficiency.

3. Enhanced Reasoning and Planning:

Chain-of-Thought and Beyond: Research continues to explore more sophisticated prompting techniques and model architectures that enable better reasoning, planning, and problem-solving.

Tool Use: Enabling LLMs to use external tools like calculators, search engines, and APIs to perform complex tasks and access external knowledge.

Reinforcement Learning from Human Feedback (RLHF): Using human feedback to fine-tune models to better align with human preferences and values.

4. Safety and Alignment:

Bias Mitigation: Continued focus on developing methods to identify and mitigate biases in training data and models.

Factuality and Grounding: Improving the ability of LLMs to generate factual and grounded information. Connecting LLMs to knowledge bases and external data sources is a key area of research.

Controllability and Steering: Developing methods to better control and steer the behavior of LLMs, ensuring they generate safe and appropriate responses.

5. Long Context Handling:

Beyond Fixed Context Windows: Research is exploring methods to overcome the limitations of fixed context windows, allowing LLMs to process and retain information from much longer sequences of text.

Attention Mechanisms and Memory Mechanisms: New attention mechanisms and memory architectures are being developed to enable more efficient processing of long contexts.

6. Personalization and Customization:

Adapting to Individual Users: Developing methods to personalize LLMs to individual users based on their preferences, history, and context.

User-Specific Fine-Tuning: Allowing users to easily fine-tune models on their own data to create highly personalized AI assistants or tools.

7. Open-Source and Community Development:

Continued Growth of Open-Source Models: The open-source community plays a crucial role in the development and advancement of LLMs. We expect to see continued growth in the availability of open-source models, tools, and resources.

Collaboration and Knowledge Sharing: Increased collaboration and knowledge sharing among researchers and developers will accelerate progress in the field.

These emerging trends are driving the rapid advancement of LLMs and opening up exciting new possibilities for their applications. As research continues, we can expect to see even more impressive capabilities and innovative uses for these powerful AI models.

10.3 The Impact of LLMs on Society and the Future of AI

Large Language Models (LLMs) are poised to have a profound impact on society and reshape the future of AI. Their capabilities in understanding and generating human language have the potential to transform various aspects of our lives, both positively and negatively.

Potential Positive Impacts:

Enhanced Communication and Accessibility: LLMs can facilitate communication across languages, making information and services more accessible to a global audience. They can also assist people with disabilities, such as by providing text-to-speech and speech-to-text capabilities.

Increased Productivity and Automation: LLMs can automate various tasks involving text processing, such as writing reports, summarizing documents, and generating emails, freeing up human time for more creative and strategic work.

Improved Education and Learning: LLMs can provide personalized tutoring, generate educational content, and assist with research, making learning more accessible and engaging.

Accelerated Scientific Discovery: LLMs can analyze large amounts of scientific literature and data, helping researchers identify patterns, generate hypotheses, and accelerate scientific breakthroughs.

Enhanced Creativity and Entertainment: LLMs can be used to generate creative content, such as stories, poems, music, and art, opening up new possibilities for artistic expression and entertainment.

Improved Customer Service and Support: LLMs can power chatbots and virtual assistants that provide instant and personalized customer service and support.

Potential Negative Impacts and Challenges:

Misinformation and Disinformation: LLMs can be used to generate realistic and convincing fake news, propaganda, and other forms of misinformation, potentially eroding trust in information sources and destabilizing societies.

Job Displacement: The automation potential of LLMs could lead to job displacement in certain sectors, particularly those involving routine text processing tasks.

Bias and Discrimination: LLMs can perpetuate and amplify biases present in their training data, leading to unfair or discriminatory outcomes.

Privacy Concerns: The use of LLMs can raise privacy concerns, particularly if they are trained on sensitive personal data.

Security Risks: LLMs can be exploited for malicious purposes, such as generating spam, phishing emails, or malicious code.

Dependence and Deskilling: Over-reliance on LLMs could lead to a decline in human skills related to writing, critical thinking, and problem-solving.

Ethical Concerns: The use of LLMs raises various ethical questions related to authorship, ownership, and the potential for misuse.

The Future of AI and the Role of LLMs:

LLMs are likely to play a central role in the future of AI, driving advancements in various areas:

Natural Language Understanding and Generation: LLMs will continue to improve in their ability to understand and generate human language, leading to more natural and intuitive human-computer interactions.

Multimodal AI: The integration of LLMs with other modalities will lead to more comprehensive and versatile AI systems that can understand and interact with the world in more human-like ways.

General-Purpose AI: LLMs are a step towards more general-purpose AI systems that can perform a wide range of tasks without requiring specialized training for each task.

Navigating the Future:

To maximize the positive impacts of LLMs and mitigate the negative ones, it's crucial to:

Promote Responsible AI Development and Deployment: Adhere to ethical guidelines and best practices for developing and deploying LLMs.

Invest in Research on Bias Mitigation and Safety: Continue research on methods to identify and mitigate bias, improve factuality, and ensure the safety of LLMs.

Foster Public Dialogue and Education: Engage in public dialogue about the potential impacts of LLMs and educate the public about their capabilities and limitations.

Develop Appropriate Regulations and Policies: Develop appropriate regulations and policies to govern the use of LLMs and address potential risks.

The future of AI with LLMs is full of both promise and challenges. By approaching their development and deployment responsibly, we can harness their power for the benefit of society while mitigating potential risks.

www.ingramcontent.com/pod-product-compliance
Lightning Source LLC
LaVergne TN
LVHW051739050326
832903LV00023B/1005